Contrasting Localities

Tell me about... Wales

Sioned Hughes and Colin Isaac

@ebol

Published in 2013 by Atebol Cyfyngedig, Fagwyr Buildings, Llandre, Aberystwyth, Ceredigion SY24 5AQ
www.atebol.com

ISBN: 978-1-908574-97-8

Edited by Colin Isaac and Ffion Eluned Owen
Additional material by Colin Isaac, Ffion Eluned Owen and Glyn Saunders Jones

Interactive activities prepared by Colin Isaac and Nudd Lewis

Designed by Ceri Jones, **stiwdio@ceri-talybont.com**
Maps designed by Alison Davies, **www.themappingcompany.co.uk**
Funded by the Welsh Government

Acknowledgments and copyright
The publishers would like to thank the following for the use of photographs and copyright material. Every effort has been made to locate the copyright owners of material used in this book. Any errors and omissions brought to the notice of the publisher with be rectified in subsequent printings.
Alamy: 3 (lower left), 40 (lower left); **©Brecon Beacons NPA:** 6 (top right), 30 (middle right), 32 (all images), 35 (right); **©Crown copyright: Royal Commission on the Ancient and Historical Monuments of Wales:** 22 (top); **Dafydd Saunders Jones:** 24 (left), 44 (lower right); **Degtyaryov Andrey/Shutterstock.com:** 29 (lower left); **Ffion Eluned Owen:** 8 (lower left); **Forestry Commission Wales:** 39 (right); **Getty Images:** 4 (lower left); **Halen Môn/Anglesey Sea Salt:** 27 (middle right); **Iestyn Hughes:** 6 (lower right), 7 (top 4), 10 (middle right), 11 (middle left, lower left), 12 (middle right, middle left), 13 (all images), 14 (main), 16 (lower left, lower right), 19 (middle right), 23 (right, lower left), 28 (lower), 45 (main), 46 (main); **Ifor Williams Trailers Limited:** 25 (left); **Llaeth y Llan Cyf/Village Dairy Ltd:** 27 (middle left); **Melin Tregwynt:** 25 (top right); **©Pembrokeshire Coast NPA:** 33 (logo); **Pen-y-Dre Farm:** 26 (main); **Photo Library Wales:** 4 (middle right), 7 (lower left), 8 (middle right), 10 (lower left), 17 (top right, lower left), 19 (main, middle), 22 (lower), 23 (top left), 27 (top right), 29 (main), 33 (middle right), 36 (lower right), 43 (middle), 44 (middle right, lower left), 45 (lower), 42 (main); **South Caernarfon Creameries Ltd Wales:** 27 (top left); **©Snowdonia National Park Authority (SNPA):** 5 (middle right), 6 (top left, middle right), 30 (top right), 31 (logo); **Tomos Watkin Award Winning Brewery:** 27 (lower left); **Thor Jorgen Udvand/Shutterstock.com:** 29 (middle right); **Urdd Gobaith Cymru:** 14 (left 3), 15 (all images), 16 (main), 18 (all images), 21 (all images), 41 (all images).
The publishers would also like to thank **©Crown copyright (2013) Visit Wales.**

Wales

Where is Wales?

Where in the world is Wales?

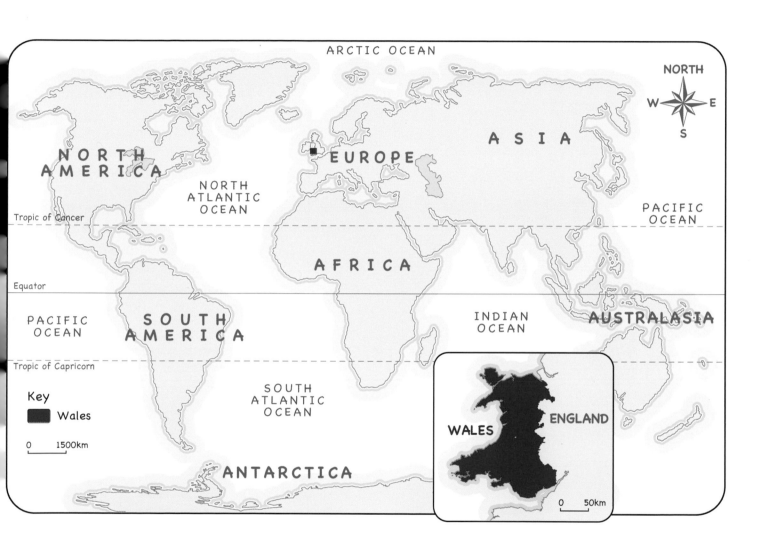

ARCTIC OCEAN

NORTH

NORTH
AMERICA

EUROPE

ASIA

NORTH
ATLANTIC
OCEAN

PACIFIC
OCEAN

Tropic of Cancer

AFRICA

Equator

PACIFIC
OCEAN

SOUTH
AMERICA

INDIAN
OCEAN

AUSTRALASIA

Tropic of Capricorn

Key

Wales

0   1500km

SOUTH
ATLANTIC
OCEAN

WALES   ENGLAND

0   50km

ANTARCTICA

Activity

1 Using the map above and/or an atlas and/or a globe and/or Google Earth on the web, describe the location of Wales in relation to the world.
2 Describe the location of Wales in relation to Europe. (What are the nearest countries?)
3 Describe the location of your local area in relation to Wales. (Which part of Wales? What are the nearest villages and towns to your local area?) You may include a map to help you.

Wales

Where is Wales?

Where is Wales in the United Kingdom?

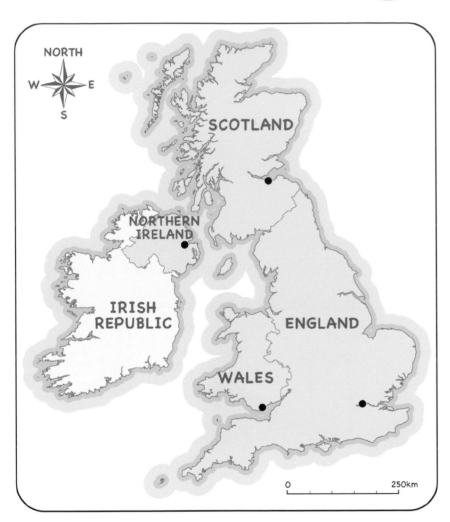

NORTH
W E
S

SCOTLAND

NORTHERN IRELAND

IRISH REPUBLIC

ENGLAND

WALES

0   250km

The creation of the United Kingdom

There are 4 countries in the United Kingdom - Wales, England, Scotland and Northern Ireland. The 4 countries were united at different times. Wales and England were united during the Tudor Period by Henry VIII. Scotland was added in 1707. Northern Ireland became part of the United Kingdom in 1921.

The National Eisteddfod of Wales

Welsh rugby team celebrating

Activity

1. Do some research to find out in which year Wales and England were united.
2. Use reference books and/or the internet to find the flags of the four countries of the United Kingdom. Copy the flags.
3. Describe the location of Wales in relation to the United Kingdom.
4. The location of the capital cities of the four countries of the United Kingdom is shown on the map. Name each of these capital cities. Use reference books and/or the internet to find out the population of each capital city. Then place these cities in order of the size of the population.

Wales

What kind of place is Wales?

What kind of landscape does Wales have?

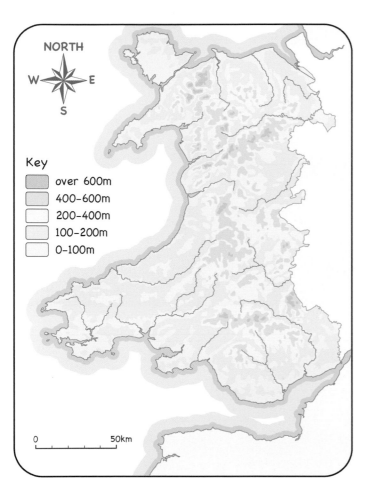

Key

- over 600m
- 400–600m
- 200–400m
- 100–200m
- 0–100m

0   50km

Wales is a mountainous country with large areas of land higher than 150 metres. In north Wales Snowdon, the highest mountain in Wales and England, is 1085 metres. In south Wales Pen y Fan, the highest mountain in the Brecon Beacons, is 886 metres.

Llyn Mymbyr and the Snowdon horseshoe

Activity

1 Discuss with a partner how the landscape affects you and the way you live. (Do you live in a rural area or an urban area? How do you travel? How does the landscape affect what you do?)

2 Write some of the ideas you have discussed on *Post-it* notes. Then compare your *Post-it* notes with those of other children in a group or class discussion. Use the notes to create a thinking map on how the landscape affects our lives.

Caernarfon and the mountains of Eryri

Wales

What kind of place is Wales?

What natural features are found in Wales?

Natural features are features that have been created by natural processes, e.g. cliff.

Activity

1 Name the natural features shown in the photographs on this page.
2 INTERACTIVE: Your teacher will give you a list of definitions of natural features and names of natural features. Link each definition to the correct name.
3 List three natural features that are found in your local area. How do these natural features affect the way people live?

Wales
What kind of place is Wales?

What human features are found in Wales?

Human features are features that have been built by people, e.g. church.

Activity

1 Name the human features shown in the photographs on this page.
2 List five other human features not shown in these photographs.
3 Name human features found in your local area.
4 Use the printed form your teacher will give you to write a paragraph describing the human features in your local area.

Wales

What kind of place is Wales?

What kind of weather does Wales have?

Caerphilly Castle

The weather in Wales is very changeable. There may be rain every month of the year but usually the months from October to January are the wettest. It's drier around the coast and wetter on the mountains.

People in Wales complain about the rain, but the weather in Wales is not as wet as in some other areas of the world. Wales does not have the extremes of weather some countries have (e.g. extremely wet or extremely dry for long periods).

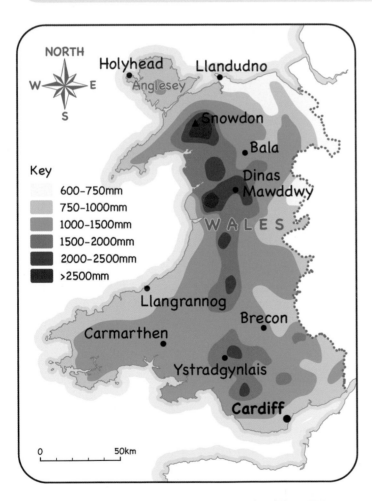

NORTH
W E
S

Holyhead
Anglesey
Llandudno
Snowdon
Bala
Dinas Mawddwy
W A L E S
Llangrannog
Brecon
Carmarthen
Ystradgynlais
Cardiff

Key
600–750mm
750–1000mm
1000–1500mm
1500–2000mm
2000–2500mm
>2500mm

0   50km

Activity

1 Various places are shown on the map opposite. List these in order of the rainfall they receive, putting the place with the highest rainfall at the top of the list and the place with the lowest rainfall at the bottom of the list.

2 Using the map and other sources, collect information about rainfall in your local area. Prepare a graph or table to show the amount of rainfall that your local area receives every year. Use this information to show which are the wettest and driest months in your area.

3 CHALLENGE: Some areas in Wales have more rain than other areas. Suggest two reasons for this.

Aberystwyth

Wales

What kind of place is Wales?

What kind of weather does Wales have?

Weather averages for Wales:	Jan	Feb	Mar	Apr	May	Jun	Jul	Aug	Sep	Oct	Nov	Dec
Temperature (°C)	4.5	4.4	6.0	8.0	11.1	14.0	16.0	15.9	14.0	11.2	7.4	5.6
Rainfall (mm)	90.6	64.3	73.3	52.3	62.3	64.6	69.0	76.6	82.5	92.7	98.1	94.5

Activity

Study the table above. Find:
a) the three wettest months;
b) the three driest months;
c) the three warmest months;
d) the three coldest months.
Use data from the table to support your answers.

	Bala	Holyhead	Llangrannog	Cardiff
Average maximum temperature (°C)	12.3	15.0	12.3	13.5
Average minimum temperature (°C)	4.3	5.5	7.1	6.8
Average annual rainfall (mm)	1100	790	870	983

Snowdon Mountain Railway in the fog

Activity

Study the table above.
1 (a) Which location has the highest average annual rainfall? (b) Which location has the highest average maximum temperature?
2 Your teacher will show you cartoons with two people making different statements about the weather in Wales. In each case, choose the statement you think is correct. Give reasons for your choice.

Activity

1 Describe the weather in your local area *today*.
2 CHALLENGE: Build up a weather diary by keeping a record of the weather in your local area every day over a particular period (e.g. a month, a term or even a year).
3 Give examples of the way the weather changes throughout the year and how these changes can affect your activities (e.g. cycling, sport).

Wales

How do people travel to Wales and in Wales?

How do people travel to Wales?

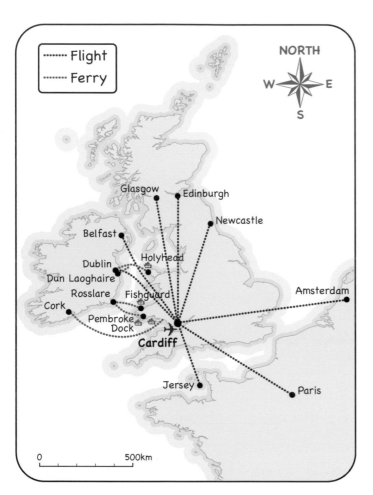

Flight
Ferry

NORTH
W — E
S

Glasgow
Edinburgh
Newcastle
Belfast
Holyhead
Dublin
Dun Laoghaire
Rosslare
Fishguard
Amsterdam
Cork
Pembroke Dock
Cardiff
Jersey
Paris

0   500km

Activity

1 Study the photographs. List the different methods of travelling to Wales. Arrange them in your order of preference, starting with the method you like best and ending with the one you like least.
2 INTERACTIVE: Answer the interactive question your teacher will give you on travel to Wales.
3 CHALLENGE: Do some research in order to name as many places as you can that have direct scheduled flights to Cardiff.

How do people travel in Wales?

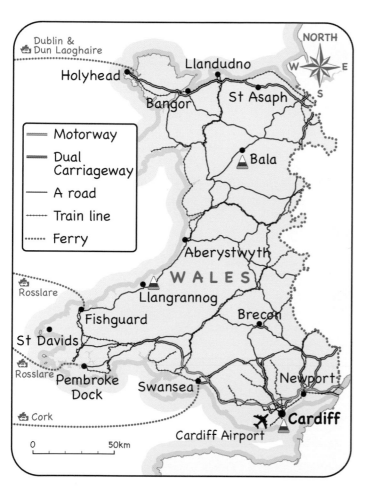

Activity

1 Some children from your school are going to the Urdd camp in Cardiff. Suggest different ways of travelling from your school to Cardiff. Which of these do you think is the best way to get there?

2 Other children from your school are going to the Urdd camp in Bala. Suggest different ways of travelling from your school to Bala. Which of these do you think is the best way to get there?

3 Suggest some advantages of people using buses rather than cars for journeys in Wales. Suggest some disadvantages of using buses rather than cars.

4 CHALLENGE: Do a survey of how people in your class/school travel to and from school each day. Show your results on a chart. Suggest ways of making travel to and from school more sustainable.

Wales

How do people travel to Wales and in Wales?

How do people travel in Wales?

How do people travel from Bangor in north Wales to Cardiff in south Wales?

Method of travel	Car	Bus	Train
Bangor-start time	08.00	09.00	07.06
Cardiff-arrive time	12.18	17.30	11.15
Total travel time	4 hours 18 minutes	8 hours 30 minutes	4 hours 9 minutes
Distance (miles/km)	185.5 miles/298.5 km		

A different way of travelling between north and south Wales is by plane between Anglesey and Cardiff. A flight leaving Anglesey at 09.05 will arrive in Cardiff at 10.00. But, of course, you will need to travel from Bangor to Anglesey before flying and from Cardiff airport to Cardiff city centre.

Activity

1 Look at the data in the table above. What is (a) the fastest way of travelling from Bangor to Cardiff and (b) the slowest way of travelling from Bangor to Cardiff? Use data to support your answer.
2 Which method of travelling has the least impact on the environment? Explain why you think this.
3 What other factors, apart from time, can affect the choice of how people travel from Bangor to Cardiff (or from Cardiff to Bangor)?
4 CHALLENGE: Do research to compare the costs of different ways of travelling from Bangor to Cardiff. (Remember: costs will be different for small cars and big cars.)

Wales

Where do people live in Wales?

Where is Llangrannog?

Some people live in rural areas in Wales. Some people live in urban areas. Others live in coastal areas.

Llangrannog is a seaside village on the Ceredigion coast. The village developed with the growth in sea trade. Several ships were built in the village and until the early 20th century most of the men in the village were sailors.

St Mary's Well
Pilgrims came to St Mary's Well to drink the water. Many people thought that the water improved their health. The well is as old as the village.

Y Gerwn
Y Gerwn is a waterfall. Years ago they used the waterfall to power a woollen mill. There are examples of the mill's products in the National Wool Museum in Drefach Felindre, Carmarthenshire.

Carreg Bica
Carreg Bica is a large rock, or stack, in the sea. It used to be part of the coast years ago before the sea attacked the coast. Some people call Carreg Bica 'the tooth of the giant Bica' – the giant spat the tooth out after suffering from toothache!

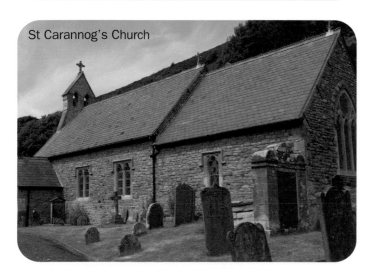
St Carannog's Church

Carreg Bica and the statue of St Carannog

St Carannog's Church
The church was built of wood about 500 A.D. On the northern side of the cemetery above the church is Cranogwen's grave.

Activity
In small groups search for information about Sarah Jane Rees (Cranogwen). Who was she? When did she live? Where did she live? What did she do? Why is she still remembered? Write a paragraph giving some information about her.

Wales

Where do people live in Wales?

What else is in Llangrannog?

Gwersyll yr Urdd
Llangrannog

One of the Urdd camps is in Llangrannog. This camp is one of the main residential centres in Wales. Thousands of children go there each year.

Activity

1 Using the photographs and comments shown on this page and the next page and/or the camp's website and/or what you can remember about the camp if you have been there, list seven activities children can do in the camp.

2 Your teacher will give the class a list of ten of these activities. Individually, list these ten activities in order of your preference. Then give the teacher your lists, so that a class list can be drawn up showing the preferences of the whole class.

3 Your teacher will give you part of a diary giving an account of a child's visit to the camp. Answer the questions your teacher will give you.

4 Write a diary of one week of your current school term or one week of the next school holiday.

Wales

Where do people live in Wales?

What else is in Llangrannog?

Llangrannog is so different to Merthyr, where I live. The coast is spectacular and the wildlife is really special. I have even seen the Bottlenose Dolphin which is special to Cardigan Bay.

I love coming with my friends to the Urdd Camp at Llangrannog. It's a great place to practise my Welsh.

My friend and I went horse riding on Wednesday. We had a fantastic time riding, feeding and grooming the horses.

Llangrannog is great! I really enjoy being with my friends on the ski slope.

Wales

Where do people live in Wales?

What kind of place is Llangrannog today?

Here are some of the things to be found in the village:

- two pubs – 'Pentre Arms' and 'The Ship'
- two cafes/restaurants – 'Patio Café' and 'The Beach Hut' (previously 'Y Gegin Fach')
- one general store – 'Glynafon'
- St Carannog Church

Patio Café

Glynafon Store

Activity

1 Draw a simple map/plan of the village of Llangrannog. Show the location of the places mentioned on this page.
2 Compare your local area with Llangrannog.

Wales

Where do people live in Wales?

Where is Bala?

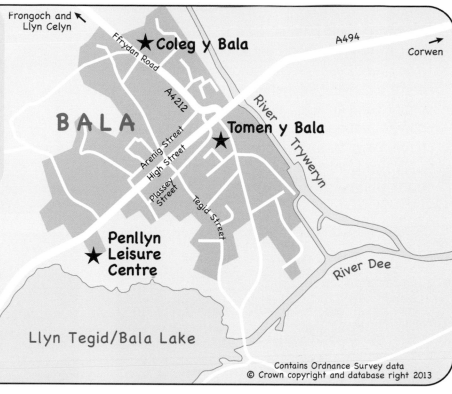

Some people live in towns in Wales. Bala is a town in Gwynedd in north-west Wales. Bala is 17 miles (27 km) to the north-east of Dolgellau and is located in the Snowdonia National Park. If somebody wants to reach Bala from Manchester International Airport it's a 1½ hour journey by car.

Frongoch and Llyn Celyn

Ffrydan Road

★ Coleg y Bala

A494

Corwen

A4212

BALA

River Tryweryn

★ Tomen y Bala

Arenig Street
High Street
Plassey Street
Tegid Street

NORTH
W E
S

★ Penllyn Leisure Centre

A494

River Dee

0   500m

Glan Llyn Camp and Dolgellau

Llyn Tegid/Bala Lake

Contains Ordnance Survey data
© Crown copyright and database right 2013

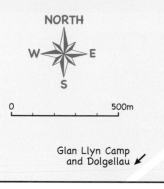
Bala and Llyn Tegid/Bala Lake

Bala is well-known for its watersports facilities, fishing, walking, cycling and a steam railway between Bala and Llanuwchllyn.

River Tryweryn

Llyn Tegid, or Bala Lake, is the largest natural lake in Wales. A unique type of fish is found there, the *Gwyniad*, a type of freshwater herring.

Activity

Design a poster to attract a family with children, parents and grandparents to visit Bala.

Wales

Where do people live in Wales?

What else is in Bala?

Gwersyll yr Urdd
Glan-llyn

One of the Urdd camps, Gwersyll Glan-llyn, is located on the southern shores of Llyn Tegid/Bala Lake. It's an outdoor education centre arranging educational courses for schools and colleges and holidays for children, young people and families. Many children and young people go to the camp to receive training and take part in water sports and outdoor activities.

Activity

1 Look at the website **www.urdd.org/glan-llyn** and list the 10 reasons for visiting Glan-llyn.
2 List activities children can do at the Glan-llyn camp.
3 Arrange these activites on the diamond-ranking sheet your teacher will give you in order to show your preferences.

Wales

Where do people live in Wales?

What is a city?

Some people live in **cities** in Wales.

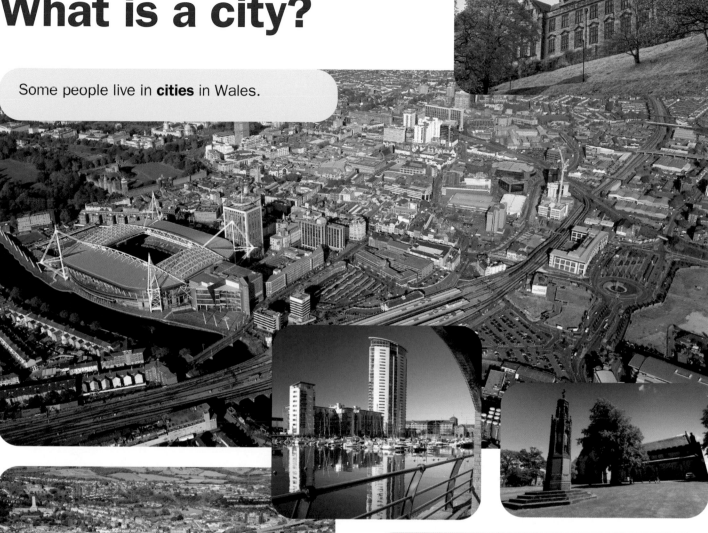

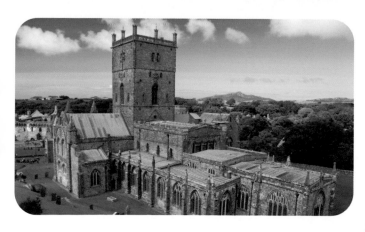

Activity

1 Name each of the Welsh cities shown in the photographs on this page.

2 INTERACTIVE: Where are the Welsh cities located? Show this on the interactive map of Wales. How close were you to the correct locations?

3 What makes a city? List the conditions which must be satisfied in order to be a city.

4 Why do some people prefer to live in cities and urban areas rather than rural areas?

5 Why do some people prefer to live in rural areas rather than cities and urban areas?

Wales

Where do people live in Wales?

What kind of place is Cardiff?

Many Welsh people live in Cardiff, the capital city of Wales.

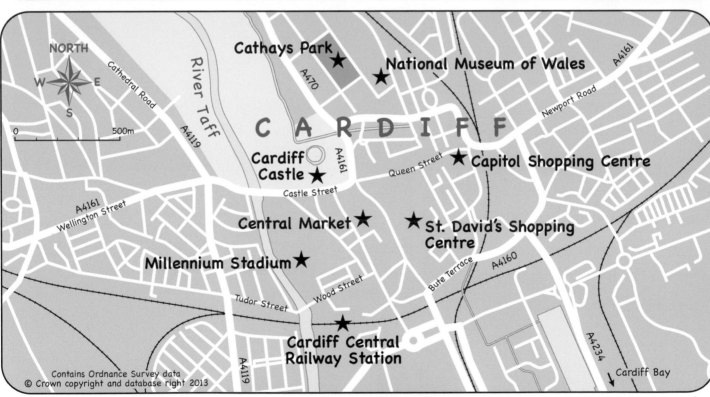

Wales Millennium Centre

City Hall and National Museum

Cardiff Castle

Activity

1 Using the map above, reference books and websites, give a description of the city of Cardiff.

2 Give reasons for and against Cardiff being a good choice as the capital city of Wales.

Wales

Where do people live in Wales?

Gwersyll yr Urdd
Caerdydd

Where is the Urdd Camp in Cardiff?

Another Urdd camp is within the Wales Millennium Centre in Cardiff. There is room for 153 people to stay in en-suite rooms and an opportunity to visit all sorts of places in and around Cardiff.

Enjoying outside the Senedd

Visiting the Millennium Stadium

Activity

1 Draw a simple map or plan to show the location of the Millennium Centre in Cardiff Bay. Show other important buildings and interesting places to see. For more information search the Urdd website **www.urdd.org/cardiff**

2 Design a poster showing the attractions in Cardiff Bay. Use sketch maps and images to make sure that the poster will attract people to the area.

3 Draw a similar poster showing interesting places to see and activities to do in your local area.

Wales

Where do people live in Wales?

How has Cardiff changed?

Cardiff has changed a great deal over the years. Many of the people who live in Cardiff now have seen many changes and developments there during their lifetime.

Cardiff Bay in 1925

Cardiff Bay today

Wales

Where do people live in Wales?

How has Cardiff changed?

Modern city centre

View from Cardiff Castle

The old and new at Cardiff Bay

The Millennium Stadium, the national stadium of Wales, was opened in 1999

Activity

1 Look at the 2 photographs on page 22 showing some of the changes that have taken place in Cardiff. List the differences you can see.
2 If you have been to Cardiff, how did you go there? What did you do there?
3 CHALLENGE: You have the opportunity to go to Cardiff next weekend. Look at the collection of photographs on the DVD and arrange activities to do during the weekend.

Wales

Where do people work in Wales?

Farming

Farming is important in Wales even though fewer people farm today. Some people farm sheep and cattle. Other farmers rear pigs or goats while others keep more exotic animals such as llamas or guanacos!

Guanacos in Pembrokeshire

Today, many farms in Wales are larger. Smaller farms are being joined with larger farms. Bigger tractors and farm implements are needed to farm the larger farms.

Silage harvesting

Activity

1 List the different kinds of farming in Wales. If there are farms in your area, what kind of farms are they?

2 Use books and/or the internet to find out how farming has changed in Wales over the years. How do you think farming will change in the future?

Wales

Where do people work in Wales?

Farming

Sheep

There are many sheep farms in Wales. These provide wool and also Welsh lamb which is famous all over the world. Originally, people would treat the wool in their homes and then make clothes with the wool.

Mills also used the wool. The mills were usually situated by rivers. The water from the river would turn the wheel and the wheel would then turn the machines in the mill.

The mills of Wales are very different today. For example, Melin Tregwynt in Pembrokeshire makes household goods such as cushions, blankets, socks, jackets, hats, scarves and bags.

Traditional Welsh wools produced at Melin Tregwynt

Daffodils

Some farms in Wales grow different crops. Some farmers grow flowers such as daffodils. A farm near Brecon grows daffodils to prepare new medicines.

Ifor Williams Trailers

Trailers

Farmers transport their animals to the markets in a trailer or lorry. Ifor Williams Trailers is a Welsh company that manufactures trailers and sells them all over the world.

Activity

Ifor Williams Trailers sell trailers all over the world. Suggest advantages of selling to other countries.

25

Wales

Where do people work in Wales?

How are some farms changing?

Some farms have decided to add to what they already do or change what they do. Some farms have adapted farm buildings to provide holiday cottages for visitors. Other farms provide Bed & Breakfast or camping facilities for visitors. Visitors enjoy staying on farms.

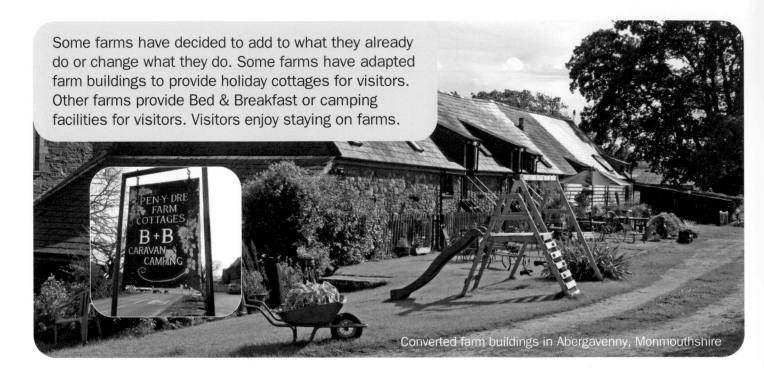

Converted farm buildings in Abergavenny, Monmouthshire

Some farmers grow organic crops or rear their animals organically. Wales is famous for producing a range of excellent dairy products and crops. These are sold in local shops, supermarkets and local farmers markets.

Activity

Your family is thinking of spending a week of your summer holiday on a farm which now keeps visitors. Give reasons why you think this would be a good idea and reasons why you think it would be a bad idea.

Activity

List different kinds of organic foods which are grown or produced in Wales.

How are some farms changing?

The food industry is a very important part of the Welsh economy …

Cheese and yoghurt from Wales
South Caernarfon Creameries in north-west Wales uses milk from local farms to make various types of cheese. The cheese is sold under the Dragon label. Llaeth y Llan Village Dairy in north-east Wales has been producing yoghurt since the 1980s. They produce several different flavours of yoghurt.

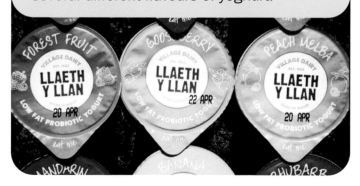

Drinks from Wales
These include cider, fruit juice, Penderyn whisky, tea and Tomos Watkin beer.

Water from Wales
Tŷ Nant bottled water from Bethania, Ceredigion, is sold in over 40 countries. The company was established in 1989 and by now its blue bottles are well known across the world. They are often seen in films and television programmes.

Salt from Wales
The Anglesey Sea Salt Company (Halen Môn) from Anglesey, north Wales, sells different flavoured salt. The company sells a variety of flavours including vanilla and celery flavoured salt!

Activity

1 Create a poster advertising one of the products mentioned on this page. You need to think of a 'catchy' phrase for the product.
2 CHALLENGE: Why have the companies mentioned on this page been successful? How do they advertise their products?

Wales

Where do people work in Wales?

New ... interesting ... exciting work!

The types of work which people in Wales do are changing. Here are a few examples.

Solar panels

In recent years, companies which manufacture and install solar panels have been established in Wales. They install solar panels on houses and other buildings. People who have solar panels installed are able to sell electricity to the national grid.

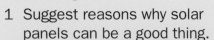
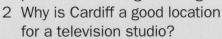

Roath Lock, the new BBC Cymru Wales drama studios in Porth Teigr, Cardiff Bay

Film and television

The film and television industry is an important industry in Wales today. Programmes such as Dr Who, Casualty, Holby City and Pobol y Cwm are filmed in a new BBC studio in Cardiff Bay. Many people work in the new studio. The Tardis from Dr Who is sometimes seen in popular places in Cardiff such as the Millennium Centre.

www.porthteigr.com/en/home

Activity

1 Suggest reasons why solar panels can be a good thing.
2 Why is Cardiff a good location for a television studio?
3 CHALLENGE: Try to discover the names of films that have been partly or wholly filmed in Wales.

Wales
Where do people work in Wales?

Aircraft industry

The Airbus factory in Broughton, north-east Wales, makes wings for aircraft. About 6,000 people work here.

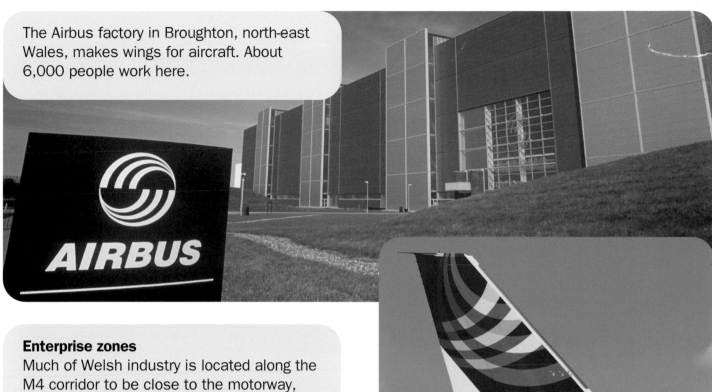

Enterprise zones
Much of Welsh industry is located along the M4 corridor to be close to the motorway, England and other countries. The government also gave grants to companies which established there.
The government is trying to do the same today. In order to encourage companies to locate in Wales they have provided money to create 5 enterprise zones in Wales.

The 5 enterprize zones are:
- Anglesey: Energy
- Cardiff: Financial Services
- Deeside: Advanced Manufacturing
- Ebbw Vale: Advanced Manufacturing
- St Athan: Aerospace

Activity
CHALLENGE: What is needed when locating a large aircraft factory such as Broughton?

Activity
1 Conduct a survey of jobs in your local area. Which jobs are the most common? Why?
2 CHALLENGE: Imagine that you are starting a new business. What business would you choose? Where would you locate the business? Give your reasons.

Wales

What are the national parks in Wales?

What is a national park?

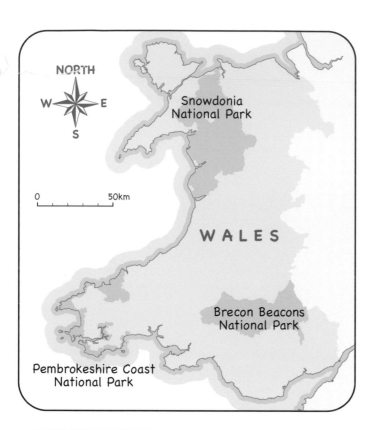

A national park is a park created by the government of a country. The purpose of national parks is caring for the environment. There are many national parks in the world.

Tal-y-llyn, Snowdonia

Cycling in the Brecon Beacons

Some of the features of a national park are: countryside towns, mountains, a wide variety of plants and animals, rivers, caves, varied scenery, forests, castles, hills and waterfalls.

The 3 national parks in Wales cover over 20% of the land area of Wales.

Barafundle Bay, Pembrokeshire Coast

Activity

1 Look at the map and describe the location of Wales's national parks.
2 Using the 'talk partners' strategy, note what you know about the national parks in Wales. Suggest what these national parks are trying to do.
3 CHALLENGE: Research the location of a national park in another country and what happens there, e.g. in the USA (e.g. Yellowstone National Park) or in Botswana (see Contrasting Localities: Tell me about... Botswana). Compare this national park with one of the national parks in Wales.

Wales

What are the national parks in Wales?

Snowdonia National Park

SNOWDONIA NATIONAL PARK

Snowdon Lily (*Lloydia serotina*)

Snowdon Mountain Railway train reaching the summit

Snowdonia National Park covers 840 square miles or 2,171 square km. It stretches from Cardigan Bay in the west to the Conwy Valley in the east and from the River Dovey in the south to the Conwy Bay coast in the north. Wales's highest mountain is in Snowdonia National Park. Its name is Snowdon and it is 1085m high. The Snowdon Lily is a rare alpine plant that is found only on Snowdon and in the area around Snowdon.

Snowdon Mountain Railway Ticket Prices

	Llanberis-summit – return	Llanberis-summit – single	Llanberis- Clogwyn* – return	Llanberis- Clogwyn* – single
Adult	£27.00	£20.00	£21.00	£17.00
Child	£18.00	£15.00	£13.00	£11.00
Disabled adult	£24.00	£17.00	£18.00	£14.00
Disabled child	£15.00	£12.00	£10.00	£8.00

(*Clogwyn – mid way up Snowdon)   www.snowdonrailway.co.uk/times_prices.php

Hafod Eryri

Activity

1 Look at the photographs and the information on this page and search for more information on the Snowdonia National Park website. Prepare a brochure showing interesting information about Snowdonia National Park.

2 Look at the table above. How much would a family with 2 adults, 1 disabled child and 2 other children have to pay to go from Llanberis to the summit and back again to Llanberis? Think of more questions based on the table, then ask your partner to answer your questions.

Wales

What are the national parks in Wales?

BRECON BEACONS
NATIONAL PARK

Brecon Beacons National Park

The Brecon Beacons National Park stretches 15 miles (24 km) from north to south and 45 miles (72 km) from west to east. It contains four mountain ranges. The name comes from the central and highest range, the Brecon Beacons themselves, and in this range is the highest peak, namely Pen y Fan (886m). The other three ranges are: The Black Mountain, Fforest Fawr (the Great Forest) and the Black Mountains.

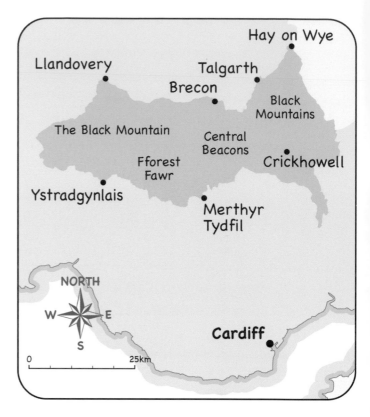

Pen y Fan

More than 32,000 people live in the National Park. About 48% of the people live in towns such as Brecon and Crickhowell.

Wild horses

Llangorse Lake

Brecon

Activity

1 How are the Brecon Beacons National Park and Snowdonia National Park similar and how are they different? Use the websites of these parks and other sources to help you.

2 CHALLENGE: It's important for a national park to keep a balance between attracting visitors and looking after the environment. Suggest rules that people should follow when visiting a national park so that they help to protect the environment.

Wales

What are the national parks in Wales?

Pembrokeshire Coast National Park

Pentre Ifan dolmen

The Pembrokeshire Coast National Park is an area of outstanding natural beauty in south-west Wales. This is Britain's only truly coastal national park. It's a stunning landscape of rugged cliffs, golden beaches, wooded estuaries and wild mountains. The Park has also a wealth of seabirds, seals and other wildlife.

Pentre Ifan

The Pentre Ifan Urdd Centre was opened in 1992. It is located about 2 miles from Newport, between Cardigan and Fishguard. The main aim of the centre is to teach children and young people about the environment. The camp building is very old, dating back to the Tudor Period. Sometimes children and young people who come to stay in Pentre Ifan get a chance to walk the Preseli Mountains and Carn Ingli.

Tenby

Pembrokeshire Coast Path

Coastal path

One special thing about the Park is the path that follows the spectacular coastline from Amroth in the south to St Dogmaels in the north. While walking along the path you can see many rocks and cliffs and fantastic views of the beaches and nearby islands. The path is 299 kilometres long. It was opened in 1970.

Activity

1 Describe the main features and main attractions of the Pembrokeshire Coast National Park. Search the Park's website to help you.
2 Copy the logos of the 3 national parks in Wales. Explain the meaning of the symbols.
3 You are staying in Pentre Ifan in December and are going to walk to Foel Cwm Cerwyn, the highest peak in the Preseli mountains. List the things you would put in your rucksack. Put them in order of importance and give reasons for your decisions.

Parc Cenedlaethol
Arfordir Penfro
Pembrokeshire Coast
National Park

Puffins

Wales
What are the national parks in Wales?

Looking after the national parks

The parks employ people to care for the environment and to ensure that the natural landscape and wildlife is conserved for the future.

Public transport at Newgale beach, Pembrokeshire

Controlling the people who visit the national parks is very important. People are encouraged to use public transport, such as buses, in order to reduce the use of cars. If there are fewer cars, there will be no need for large car parks near the beaches and other attractions.

Walking in Snowdonia

The Countryside Code
The aim of the code is to try to ensure that people will respect and protect the countryside. Here are some of the rules of the Countryside Code:

- close gates
- keep dogs on a lead
- take rubbish home
- help to keep water clean
- protect wildlife, plants and trees
- do not make unnecessary noise
- do not touch livestock, crops, farm tools
- keep to public footpaths on farmland
- use gates and stiles to cross fences, hedges and walls

Activity
Using the information on this page and suitable photographs and/or drawings make a booklet showing some of the rules of the Countryside Code.

Wales

What are the national parks in Wales?

Key
Question
6

Looking after the national parks

Interview with a warden

Ann: Thanks very much for agreeing to be interviewed.

Warden: You're welcome. I'm lucky to work as a National Park Warden.

Ann: So what exactly is your work?

Warden: My work is looking after everybody living in the park, everybody working in the park and all who visit the park.

Ann: How do you do that?

Warden: During the summer I lead walking trips for adults and school children in the park. During the winter I repair footpaths and gates.

Ann: How can walkers help to look after the paths and the park?

Warden: It's important that the walkers walk on the paths to protect plants and not spoil the landscape and the environment. It's important that everybody closes the gates in case the animals such as the sheep escape and are harmed.

Ann: Thank you very much. I have learnt a lot about a warden's work.

Problems in the park – planning

It's difficult to build new houses in a national park because of the park's strict planning rules. What about young families who want houses built within their local areas so that they do not have to move away?

Group of children with a warden

Enjoying in a national park

Activity

CHALLENGE: Read the interview with a National Park Warden shown on this page. Then write a warden's diary, describing the work he/she has done.

Activity

CHALLENGE: A company wants to build a holiday park in one of the national parks including 80 timber chalets, a swimming pool, an adventure area, cycle paths, footpaths, 3 restaurants and 1 small food shop. The developement will create 100 jobs. List some arguments for the development and some arguments against the development. You are a member of the council's planning committee. What will be your decision?

Wales

Why do people visit Wales?

Mountain biking

Why is the tourism industry important to Wales?

The tourism industry is very important to the Welsh economy. Tourism provides work for about 10% of the labour force in Wales. Tourists spend about £9 million a day on holidays in Wales, which makes a total of £3.3 billion per year.

Shopping in Beaumaris, Anglesey

Conwy Castle

Porthdinllaen, Llŷn Peninsula

Why do people come to Wales? Wales is a beautiful country with a rich history and many natural and human attractions.
www.visitwales.com

Many people come on holiday to Wales. More than a million tourists from abroad come to Wales on holiday each year. Most of the tourists come from the Irish Republic, the USA and Germany.

Activity

1 Explain why the tourism industry is important in Wales. Search for information and data that will support your answer.
2 Why might visitors visit your local area? Describe what's there to attract them and what they can do there.

Wales
Why do people visit Wales?

Where do visitors stay?

Camping and caravan holidays
Some people go camping, either on campsites or on a farm. Others stay in a caravan.

Campsite near Three Cliffs Bay, Swansea

Hotel holidays
Some people prefer to stay in a hotel with a swimming pool or spa.

Hotel near Llandudno Pier

Bed-and-breakfast/ self-catering holidays
Some visitors stay in bed-and-breakfast accommodation while on holiday in Wales. Others stay in a cottage or house where they make their own meals.

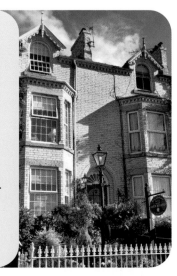

Activity
1 Draw pictures with labels to show the different kinds of places people stay in when on holiday in Wales.
2 List the hotels in your local area. List other kinds of places where visitors to your area can stay.
3 Where would you choose to visit in Wales? Where would you stay while you are there? Give reasons for your answers.

Wales

Why do people visit Wales?

What do visitors do on holiday in Wales?

Visitors do very many different activities on holiday in Wales.

Oakwood Theme Park

Attractions

There are various kinds of attractions in Wales for the various types of visitors, e.g. castles and other historic buildings, nature reserves, parks and gardens, a variety of beaches and seaside resorts, the National History Museum at St Fagans, Techniquest in Cardiff, Dan-yr-Ogof showcaves, Oakwood Theme Park, Big Pit Mining Museum, Welsh Slate Museum in Llanberis, Ffestiniog Railway, Anglesey Sea Zoo and many, many more.

Isle of Anglesey Coastal Path

Walking holidays

Some people enjoy walking holidays. There are many coastal and country footpaths in Wales. It's even possible to walk around the whole coastline of Wales!

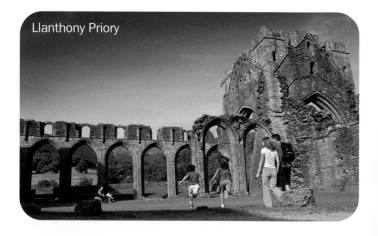
Llanthony Priory

Anglesey Sea Zoo

St Fagans

Techniquest

Activity

Suggest places in your local area which would be suitable for people who enjoy walking holidays. Give reasons for you answers.

38

Wales

Why do people visit Wales?

What do visitors do on holiday in Wales?

Adventure and sports holidays

Some people like to come to Wales to do activities such as surfing, sailboarding, white water rafting, kayaking, canoeing and sailing. Such sports are called extreme sports. Visitors go to places like Twr-y-Felin Centre on the Pembrokeshire coast and the Tryweryn Centre in Bala to do these activities.

Cycling holidays

There are many cycle paths in Wales. People can go mountain biking through forests in different places in Wales, such as the Coed y Brenin Centre near Dolgellau or Bwlch Nant yr Arian near Aberystwyth.

Coed y Brenin

Another extreme sport is coasteering – wearing a wet suit, helmet and an old pair of trainers and then swimming, climbing and jumping off the cliffs.

Other visitors like to stay in a holiday centre such as Bluestone Park in south Pembrokeshire.

Coasteering in Pembrokeshire

Activity

1 List different kinds of adventure/sports holidays available in Wales and give examples of places that provide these kinds of holidays.

2 CHALLENGE: Research to collect more information about one of the holiday centres mentioned on this page or included in your list. Then create a poster advertising the holiday.

Wales

Why do people visit Wales?

What do visitors do on holiday in Wales?

Llandudno

Holidays in the capital city
Some people like to go on holiday to the capital city in Cardiff.

The seaside
People enjoy visiting the beaches and coast of Wales. Many of the seaside towns in Wales such as Rhyl, Llandudno, Aberystwyth, Tenby and Barry are very popular.

Barry Island

Visitors arriving at Skomer Island

Advantages and disadvantages of visitors
The more visitors there are coming to Wales, the more money there is coming into the country. But also the more visitors there are, the more problems they cause, e.g damage to the countryside and traffic problems. Therefore it's important to try to ensure that visitors do not destroy the very places that they enjoy visiting.

Skomer Island
The island is a Nature Reserve. A boat brings visitors to the island in the summer. Pembrokeshire Coast National Park controls the number of people going to the island each day in the summer. They are looking after the island's wildlife by doing this.

Activity

1 Suggest reasons why some visitors like to have holidays in the capital city.
2 Suggest advantages and disadvantages of vistors coming to Wales.

40

Wales

What's special about Wales?

urdd.org

What's special about the Urdd?

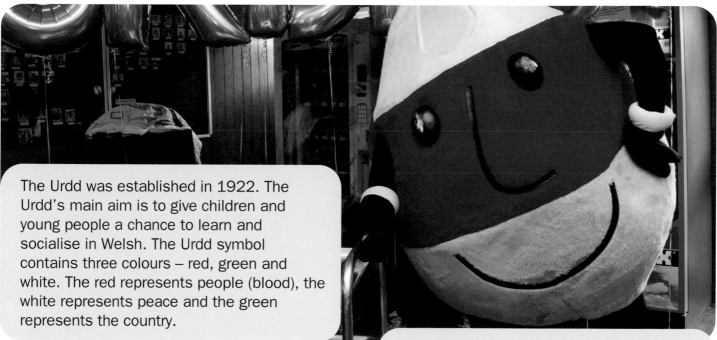

The Urdd was established in 1922. The Urdd's main aim is to give children and young people a chance to learn and socialise in Welsh. The Urdd symbol contains three colours – red, green and white. The red represents people (blood), the white represents peace and the green represents the country.

Children competing in the Urdd swimming gala

CHWARAEON YR URDD
urdd.org/chwaraeon

The Urdd offer a wide choice of activities which include:
- weekly club activities
- sport activities, e.g. rugby, football, gymnastics, swimming and athletics
- competing in an eisteddfod, e.g. dancing, singing, reciting, performing, arts and crafts
- leisure activities at the Urdd camps in Llangrannog, Glan-llyn, Pentre Ifan and Cardiff
- voluntary work overseas and meeting children and young people from other countries

Every year on 18 May the Urdd announces a Message of Peace and Goodwill from the youth of Wales to the youth of the world. In 2012, young people from Snowdonia presented the message on the summit of Snowdon.

Activity

1 Design a pamphlet showing some of the things you can do if you are a member of the Urdd. Remember to include some of the activities that happen in your area.
2 Suggest reasons why the Urdd transmits a message of goodwill every year.

Wales

What's special about Wales?

What's special about the Senedd?

The Senedd is home to the Chamber and Committee Rooms of the The National Assembly for Wales. The Senedd was opened in 2006. The National Assembly for Wales is responsible for making important decisions.

The circular debating chamber in the Senedd

The Assembly's Devolved Subject Areas

Culture	Highways and transport	Social welfare	Welsh Language
Economic development	Health and health services	Sport and recreation	National Assembly for Wales
Education and training	Fire and rescue services and fire safety	Tourism	Ancient monuments and historic buildings
Environment	Local government	Town and country planning	Agriculture, forestry, animals, plants and rural development
Food	Public administration	Water and flood defence	Housing

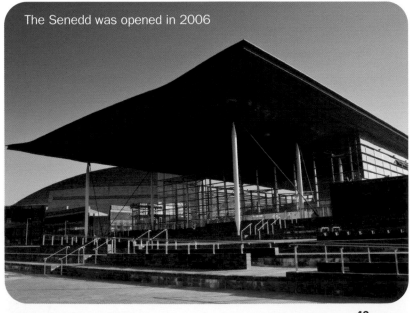

The Senedd was opened in 2006

Activity

1 What is the name of the Assembly Member who represents your area?
2 Describe three of the subject areas for which the National Assembly for Wales is responsible.
3 INTERACTIVE: List the subject areas that are in the above table in order of importance in your opinion. Explain your decisions.

42

Wales

What's special about Wales?

Is Wales a multicultural country?

My name is Simeon and I am a Jew and live in Swansea. My favourite things about Wales are the beautiful beaches, Swansea's football team and my friends.

My name is Sian and I live in Prestatyn in north-east Wales. My grandfather and grandmother and most of my relatives live in Prestatyn but I also have a grandmother in Trinidad, my father's home. My favourite things about Wales are the spectacular scenery, the wildlife and the people.

My name is Amin and I live in the Butetown area of Cardiff. I am a Muslim and I support the Welsh rugby team. My favourite thing about Wales is the castles.

My name is Talitha and I live in Newtown. My father's family come from Israel. My favourite thing about Wales is that the government is starting to care for the environment by asking people to recycle and re-use everything.

Activity

1 Read what the 4 children shown on this page say about themselves and Wales. What does this show about Wales?

2 Suggest 10 things that are important about Wales in your opinion. Give reasons for your answers.

3 CHALLENGE: Send an e-mail to a friend in another country describing your local area and Wales. In your e-mail give interesting facts about Wales and tell your friend what Wales means to you.

4 CHALLENGE: Do some research at home to find out which areas or countries your parents and grandparents come from.

Wales

What kind of energy is in Wales?

How does Wales get its energy?

There are two kinds of energy sources:
1 Non-renewable sources, such as coal, gas and oil that are going to come to an end some day.
2 Renewable sources such as wind, solar and water power that will never run out.

Wind energy

Wind energy
The power of the wind turns the blades of the turbine. This blade movement produces electricity. Wind farms are built in high and exposed areas. Some wind farms have been built in the sea, e.g. off the coast of Rhyl in north-east Wales.

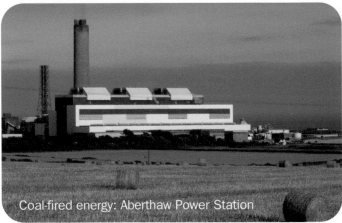
Coal-fired energy: Aberthaw Power Station

Biomass energy: Biomass energy plant, Margam

Solar energy: Talgarth

Wales

What kind of energy is in Wales?

How does Wales get its energy?

Hydroelectric energy; Nant-y-Moch, Aberystwyth

Croeso i Nant-y-Moch
Welcome to Nant-Y-Moch

Gas-fired energy:
Pembroke Power Station

Some people disagree with some energy sources. Why?

- They call energy sources such as oil, coal and gas poor/dirty energy sources.
- They call energy sources such as the wind, sun and waves clean/green energy. These energy sources do not increase the levels of CO_2 in the air. They are also called low-carbon energy.

Activity

1 List and describe different kinds of energy sources in Wales.
2 Sort the different sources of energy into 2 lists under the heading non-renewable sources and renewable sources.
3 CHALLENGE: Conduct a survey of energy sources used in the homes of the pupils in your class. Make graphs or charts to show your results.

Wales

What kind of energy is in Wales?

Are Wales's energy sources changing?

Nuclear energy

The Wylfa Power Station in Anglesey produces electricity by using a nuclear reactor. A nuclear power station in Trawsfynydd in Gwynedd has closed.

Nuclear energy: Wylfa Power Station

The Welsh Government has a plan to increase renewable energy. They aim to produce more 'green energy' from wind, solar and wave power.

The government is planning to develop more wind farms.

The Welsh Government plans to make Anglesey an energy enterprise zone. New wind farms will be built on land and in the sea. A new nuclear power station could also be built at Wylfa in the future.

Tan 8

Tan 8 is another Welsh Government plan to produce renewable 'green' energy.

- A number of wind farms will be built in mid and south Wales.
- Power lines will have to be built to move the electricity from the wind farms.
- Electricity will be supplied to other parts of the UK.
- Some people are against Tan 8. They believe that wind turbines and power lines spoil the scenery.

Activity

Some people want a new nuclear power station to be built in Wales. Suggest reasons why this might be a good thing for Wales. Suggest reasons why this might be a bad thing for Wales.

Activity

1 Suggest arguments in favour of plans like the Tan 8 Plan. Suggest arguments against plans like the Tan 8 Plan.
2 If you were responsible for making the final decision regarding these plans, what would be your decision and why?
3 CHALLENGE: The government intends building a large wind farm in your local area. Write a letter to the Assembly expressing your opinion about this wind farm. Use the framework on the DVD to help you structure your letter.

Wales

How can Wales be made sustainable?

Key
Question
10

Why do we need to make Wales a sustainable country?

In making Wales sustainable we are looking after the environment and the resources so that there will be enough resources available for people in the future. In improving services we are not wasting or overusing resources so that there will be enough available for the future.

The ARBED scheme

This scheme aims to improve more than 6000 homes in Wales so that they will use energy better. This is done in various ways, e.g. upgrading and changing boilers, wall insulation, upgrading windows, structural work and energy saving advice.

Reusable carrier bags

Litter pollution on beach

Charging for carrier bags

Since October 2011 people in Wales have had to pay at least 5p for each single-use carrier bag. This scheme aims to reduce litter, protect wildlife, save resources and reduce climate change.

Activity

1 List arguments in favour of charging for plastic bags. List arguments against charging for plastic bags. What's your opinion of this policy?
2 What is being done in your local area to help the area and Wales to be sustainable?
3 Use a 'sustainability tree' to list things that you yourself can do to help your local area and Wales to be sustainable.
4 CHALLENGE: You, as a group, are given the responsibility of making decisions on how to make your local area/Wales more sustainable. Produce a multimedia presentation to show your decisions and the reasons for these decisions.

Wales

What might happen in the future?

What might happen in Wales in the future?

I would like to see better train and bus services in Wales. I live in the countryside and so cannot use trains and buses because there's no service. I have to use the car all the time and that's costly and causes more pollution in the environment and more harm to plants and animals.

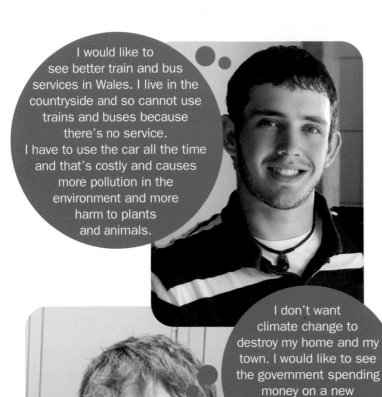

Activity

1. Imagine how Wales will have changed by 2050. Consider the following: transport, weather, way of life, the environment. List your ideas.
2. As a class, discuss your ideas and list them on a thinking map.
3. List 10 things you would put in a time capsule that would be opened sometime in the future to give the people of that period an idea of life in Wales today.

I don't want climate change to destroy my home and my town. I would like to see the government spending money on a new breakwater and wall for defence from the sea.

I don't want more wind turbines in Wales. There are enough here already and they don't produce much electricity. I'd like to see a new nuclear power station opened in Wales so that there's more work for Welsh people.

Activity

1. You are in charge of the future development of Wales. Draw up an action plan for the future which includes ways of developing tourism and helping to solve transport problems as well as protecting the country's natural environment. Make a list of actions you think should be taken and give your reasons for them.
2. In groups, discuss your individual action plans and decide on your group's action plan for developing Wales in the future.
3. Each group is to make a presentation of its action plan to the rest of the class.
4. The whole class then discusses the different action plans and decides on a final action plan for developing Wales in the future.